Richard Bassett was principal horn of the National Slovene Opera House before being appointed in 1983 the Central and Eastern Europe correspondent of *The Times*. Since the end of the Cold War he has worked in the City but has also found time to write books, including a biography of Admiral Canaris which has been translated into nine languages. He is currently writing a three-part history of the Habsburgs, *For God and Kaiser*, which will be published by Yale University Press in 2015. He is married with two children.

Works by the same author

A Guide to Central Europe
The Austrians: Strange Tales from the Vienna Woods
Waldheim and Austria
The Traveller's Companion to Vienna
(with John Lehmann)
Balkan Hours
Hitler's Spy Chief: The Wilhelm Canaris Mystery
Restoring Confidence in the Financial System
(with Sean Tully)

TRIESTE '79

✤

RICHARD BASSETT

Published by The Cuckoo Press
for John Sandoe (Books) Ltd
10 Blacklands Terrace, London SW3 2SR

© Richard Bassett 2013

The moral right of the author has been asserted

A CIP catalogue reference for this book
is available from the British Library

ISBN 978 0 9566444 5 9

Designed by Fenella Willis

Printed and bound in the UK by CPI Group (UK) Ltd
Croydon, CR0 4YY

In memory of Cornelia Kirpicsenko-Meran
(*geb.* Gräfin von Meran)
1963–2013

TRIESTE '79

There are many shades of sky-blue. In my experience, the most memorable one is that which fills the Adriatic sky around Trieste after a few days of the Bora wind. The air has a clarity that I have only seen equalled in the highlands of Tibet. From the Molo Audace, the simple slab of Istrian stone which stretches out to the sea from the Triestine Riva, the peaks of the Alps, faintly pink, can be glimpsed nearly seventy miles away to the west beyond the lagoons. To the east, the Istrian peninsula, lazy and shimmering in the sunlight, stretches like some reclining voluptuary towards the hazy and distant lands of the Quarnero. In winter it can be cold in this bright sunlight but the colours are so vivid that one scarcely feels it. 'Come to Trieste,' James Joyce once wrote to a friend, 'and you will see sun.'

One hundred years ago this June, an archduke, all too aware that his assassination had been ordered, set out from here to visit Sarajevo. Barely a week later the Dreadnought that took him away brought him and his wife back in their coffins. It is part of Trieste's spell to give the impression that time is unchanging. From the Molo, the view out to sea is the same today as it was in 1914, or for that matter in 1979 when the Simplon-Orient Express, after rattling down the cliffs beyond Duino, dropped me a few minutes' walk away one bright January morning.

I might have chosen any time in the previous or subsequent forty years to effect this arrival in Trieste and I would have been greeted by the same picture of tranquillity. Stabilised finally by an international treaty and sealed from its hinterland by the Cold War, Trieste was reduced in status to a minor Italian port. This once great commercial city – in 1914, the greatest port of the Austro-Hungarian Empire, and an entrepôt which had pioneered offshore financial prosperity long before the term had been coined – had become an enormous museum with very, very few visitors.

In 1979 I had studied the city's map from an old Baedeker of the Eastern Alps bought for fifty pence from John Ruston's splendid antiquarian bookshop near my home in Bournemouth. With it, I had managed to find my destination within fifteen minutes of walking from the station. The British School in the Via Torrebianca had placed a small but beguiling advertisement in *The Times* asking for an English teacher. Glimpsed from a dark, cold, windswept avenue on the south coast a few weeks before Christmas, the very name 'Trieste' conjured up warm romance and the chance of escape from a peculiarly English parochialism. An exchange of telegrams a month later secured the post.

I had in fact visited Trieste before. Six months earlier and fresh from university, I had taken the train from Ljubljana to Trieste. Then, as now, the Bora had just died down to reveal an azure horizon of breathtaking clarity. The effect was not just visual: it also made my spirits surge. Filled with enthusiasm and energy, I had struck up conversation with an elegant, middle-aged lady who was keen to practise her rather archaic English on a native. Thanks to her, my accommodation was arranged, I was piled up with guide books and maps, and details of the best-value restaurants were inscribed on my memory. Her inexhaustible kindness combined with the soft Imperial Viennese architecture, the bright light and the smell of superb coffee to paint an attractive picture of the old Imperial and Royal civilisation which I had observed in Prague and Vienna but which seemed far more vibrant here. It was almost as if the best of the Habsburg Empire had been bottled in this place for preservation for future generations so that, decades after the demise of the last Habsburg Emperor, a stranger might pass along its grand streets and think, 'Ah, yes, this is what an Imperial Austrian city was really like.'

On that wintry afternoon six months later, the little advertisement buried in the sober pages of the old *Times* had therefore fallen on fertile ground. It offered a chance to renew an acquaintance, mature, and learn another language. In those days it was a popular and plausible view that three years was a very short time for a university education: at Cambridge in the early 1970s, a 'career' was considered an eccentric concept. Sauntering along the Riva, I perceived Trieste to be an extension of my cultural formation, its great Ringstrasse buildings the natural culmination of the Palladian splendours which I had recently left behind.

Two days after my arrival, I went to the tobacconist's just off the main square to buy some postage stamps. As I entered, a lady with spectacles attached by wires around her neck took one look at me and hailed me with a shout of surprise. We had exchanged neither addresses nor even names six months earlier, but I could never have failed to recognise that old-fashioned grace.

'Come with me!' Mietta grabbed my arm. Chattering about the strange power of coincidence, she briskly escorted me to the small canal which flows from in front of the solemn neo-classical church of San Antonio towards the sea. It was of course another dazzlingly sunny day. As we marched along the Ponte Rosso, I remembered the difference between 'tourist' and 'traveller' that my amiable tutor, Gorley Putt, had been fond of owlishly pointing out. The former was a prisoner of superficialities, forever condemned to be ripped off and abused; the latter penetrated below the surface and could be relied upon to enjoy the places he visited to the full. To know people was essential to understanding how a foreign city worked.

Mietta smiled mischievously. 'I want you to meet some friends of mine.' Halfway along the canal, a small, unpretentious door led to a café, the Bar Danubio. The simplicity of its decoration made it very different from the grander cafés glimpsed in Vienna or Graz, or even elsewhere in Trieste. Later I would discover the opulent Specchi on the grand square and the Tommaseo with its ornate columns. All were light years away in atmosphere and style from the Bar Danubio, whose interior was painted in fading cream and was unadorned save for a small black-and-white photograph of Trieste, high on the wall, taken from the nearby clifftop at some indeterminate date between 1870 and 1970.

There could not have been more than half a dozen tables in the café, of which three were occupied. Behind the large coffee machine, the waiter was studying a crossword in the local newspaper. If there had been conversation, it ceased before we came in: the occupants were reading in a library hush.

We broke with enthusiasm into this world of cerebral calm. 'The poetess, Lina Galli.' I saw a grey-haired old lady wearing round her neck a large silver medallion which, on closer inspection, was an old Maria Theresa Thaler. She looked up from her newspaper and smiled benignly: *'Piacere.'* But before conversation could begin, Mietta pulled me to one side towards another table from which an old man with heavy-lidded eyes slowly peered at us without expression. 'And this is the writer, Giorgio

Voghera… and his friend, Piero Kern.' Voghera gave a hint of a smile. Kern, who seemed in his mid-fifties and had streaks of red in his hair, answered, 'So you are English? Have you read *King Solomon's Mines*?' Straight away he supplied his own enigmatic response: 'So! The palaver is over.' (The Anglo-Indian word was pronounced in Austrian dialect, with a stress on the first syllable.) With that, he returned to his paper.

At the third table an old woman with a handsome profile sat scrutinising a Rebus puzzle. 'And this,' said Mietta, with faintly recalibrated enthusiasm, 'is my aunt, Myrta Fulignot, the widow of the painter Guido Fulignot.' Myrta smiled radiantly; her eyes were dark, lazy, almost Oriental. I found Signora Fulignot rather easier to converse with. She spoke a soft German with an indeterminate Austrian accent.

My duties at the school were light. After the morning's teaching, on Myrta's advice I would usually go to a little restaurant near the Greek Orthodox church where Maria, a kind, portly woman, offered simple pasta and salad washed down with an irresistible quarter-bottle of Merlot from the Gorician hills a few miles away. Despite its modesty, this trattoria was not cramped: we dined under high, vaulted ceilings.

As in the Bar Danubio, simplicity entailed no discomfort. There were perhaps a dozen guests a day. One table immediately attracted attention as it was reserved without fail every lunchtime for four respectable-looking men in their early fifties. Each was dressed in a dark tweed jacket of Continental pattern with a tie, and scrupulously creased grey flannel trousers. Each place was set with its own individual miniature bottle of wine, just enough for two glasses. A faded portrait of Kaiser Franz Josef gazed benignly from above.

Unlike the other guests, these men were such regulars that they merited their own personal napkins, folded into pewter rings. I came to learn that these anonymous bureaucrats were relatively lowly employees – today they might be called middle managers – of the Generali, the great insurance company headquartered in Trieste, whose policies in Habsburg days had stretched to every corner of the Empire. A later historian argued persuasively that one could ascertain whether someone had roots in the Habsburg lands simply by asking whether they or their family had ever been insured by the Generali.

These men were quietly spoken, polite and convivial. Everything about them was understated. Although the natural partisanship of youth made me favour energy and dynamism, I could see that here was something almost enviable: the simple bureaucratic life, unhurried and closed to any events which might challenge the domestic and professional certainties of routine. These were not men who would ever confuse movement with progress. No doubt on those very rare occasions when they intervened, it was with decisive effect. As they departed promptly each day at ten to two, to head back to their offices or to a siesta, seemingly untroubled by financial or any other worries, I was unaware that I was witnessing a certain ephemeral *douceur de vivre*: men of modest means with comfortable, ordered lives, the like of which, after a few more years, I would not see again.

Voghera had worked most of his life at the Generali. Although I had not then read his autobiographical masterpiece, *Il Direttore Generale*, let alone his widely acclaimed (in Central Europe) *Il Segreto* and *Gli Anni della Psicoanalisi*, it was immediately apparent that he was an acute observer of life. These works, still unknown to an English audience, are powerfully evocative of the pre-1914 Triestine world. With their incisive analysis, they cannot be called nostalgic.

Voghera, like his writings, was a realist. Life in an insurance company had afforded him, despite his general air of untidy modesty, the financial luxury of early retirement, with enough basic material comfort to write, and to do so brilliantly.

Voghera was inscrutable at first. While he never offered the slightest protest, I often felt I was disturbing his peace and calm with my foolish questions about Trieste. Gradually, as my Italian improved, we moved away from conversing in German and he became ever more loquacious. On the topic of Trieste's railways, a subject of unceasing fascination for me, he explained how there had been three routes to Trieste from Vienna. Today there are none. The Pontebba Bahn, the Staatsbahn, the glorious Südbahn – and the engineering feats associated with them – were all described with the detail of the specialist. For Voghera, such extensive knowledge was a natural corollary of a Triestine childhood.

Voghera was knowledgeable about everything. As my Italian progressed, he urged me to use the most complicated words I could, 'as these are more or less the same usually in every language.' If I announced one day that I was going to visit Cividale, he would give me a short lecture on the civilisation of the Lombards. If I was off to

Milan for the weekend, he would caution me against the impenetrability of the local dialect and urge me to visit the courtyards of the great town palaces in the centre of the city, to enjoy their lush and secret treasures of vegetation and architecture. I should never forget, however, that in 'a great city like Milan', professional people could afford to behave less well towards each other than in a small city like Trieste where everyone knew everyone else.

Occasionally Kern would join in with some practical advice, though he was generally indifferent to my juvenile thrills of travel. He had the air of a creature I had never encountered in England in those pre-Thatcher days, a truly commercial man of the world, *'un uomo degli affari'*. He was always keen to get to the banks before they closed at midday; always complaining of the delay in the cost and transfer of money from Brazil, where, it seemed – though he never alluded to this directly – he had various interests.

Kern's great-aunt had married the father of the composer Gustav Mahler. They had both been 'teachers in a school in Bohemia'. When, with the precocity of youth, I had corrected him by pointing out that it was Moravia, not

Bohemia, Kern — typically in a deadpan voice — observed, *'Ma Lei e pedante di corrigermi su queste piccole cose.'*[1] I soon came to realise that this was characteristic of a mordant sense of humour which disguised the warmest and kindest of natures. If he asked you some question about an obscure book and you failed to know the answer, his refrain, delivered always in a voice of convincingly feigned astonishment, was *'Ma la sua ignoranza e spaventosa.'*[2] But if you dared to impart some pearl which might be seen to increase or — heaven forefend — dispute, ever so slightly, his own knowledge, you were branded an incorrigible pedant.

Once in a while, we would be joined in the Bar Danubio by a striking figure, with Homburg and red curls, who would introduce an element of energy into the café. Salmone — I never learnt his last name — was a scholar of Hebrew and clearly a man of great learning although, when I was present, he spoke in a loud, fractured German, rich in cacophonous grammatical errors and an exaggerated use of the word *'Euch'*[3]. This finally provoked the normally placid Voghera to

---

[1] 'But he is a pedant to correct me on these little details.'
[2] 'But his ignorance is terrifying.'
[3] Formal 'you'

the only mild outburst of exasperation I ever witnessed in him. Turning his penetrating gaze on this most earnest of scholars, he said with faint petulance: *'Schauen Sie, Salmone, mit diesem "Euch" kommt man nirgends hin!'*[4]

Other guests at the Bar Danubio were less conventionally cerebral. Myrta had a broad circle of friends who seemed the apogee of eastern Adriatic beauty and were utterly unlike the female company I had known at school or university. First there was Signora Corbidge, a Greek woman of Aphroditian beauty in her early thirties, with the most exquisite dark eyes and hair I have ever seen. Then there was Signora Jacobs, a blonde and elegant woman with sparkling eyes and a captivating smile. Apparently it was normal that these sophisticated women should be in so modest, even scruffy, a bar. I noticed, however, that, apart from a brief and polite exchange of greetings with Voghera and Kern, they focussed all their attention on Myrta's table.

Myrta lived in some style in a set of rooms above the canal in the old Palazzo Scaramanga,

---

4 'Look, Salmone, with this use of *'Euch'* one cannot go anywhere.' His point was that this particular use of the word was no longer current.

13

opposite the Serbian Orthodox church, whose great blue dome was visible from the windows of her salon. On the walls hung paintings by her former husband, a mixture of fashionable portraits of society women and nudes of intense sensuality. These women, with their haunting eyes and superbly curved limbs, gazed down on me from every wall. To complete this picture of feminine grace, a white-and-black top hat, made of Venetian glass, stood upside-down on the table. It acted as a vase and was filled with orchids. On my visits for tea I grew to know each of these paintings well, but it would be many months before Myrta felt sufficiently at ease to confide that the nudes were all studies of herself, made nearly half a century earlier.

One of Myrta's great distractions in life at this time was bridge. She was a member of the *Circolo del Bridge*, an institution that was an important part of Triestine life. In its fine neo-classical club rooms in the old 18th-century palace of the stock exchange, she and the consuls (mostly honorary) gathered each week to play cards and exchange the odd piece of political or commercial gossip.

An old friend in Graz gave me an introduction to one of these, the 89-year-old Honorary

French Consul in Trieste, Baron Geoffrey (or Gottfried, or Geoffredo) Banfield. Banfield certainly sounded to me then (and I have had no reason subsequently to revise my opinion) to be the most dashing man I would ever meet. He was a highly decorated former Imperial Austria flying ace, who had on countless occasions – sometimes single-handedly – defended Habsburg airspace during the First World War against vastly superior forces. It was largely due to his efforts that, right up until November 1918, not a single Allied aircraft managed to penetrate Austrian airspace during the Great War.

How Triestine that he should now be a French diplomat. How Triestine that his name, despite his many Habsburg decorations for valour, was English. In 1914, the old Habsburg Emperor Franz Josef had offered the many Belgian, French and English officers in his service safe conduct back to their countries of origin; or, if they preferred, Austrian nationality. Banfield, whose father had been an Irish officer in the Habsburg navy, had taken Austrian citizenship on graduating from the Imperial and Royal Naval Academy at Fiume along the coast. By the time he was thirty he had changed his nationality three times. His very existence testified to the durability of that generation of Triestines, survivors of an older order whose ruling multilingual oligarchy had been truly supranational.

And so it was, on yet another of those bright January mornings, that I found myself at the headquarters of the Tripcovich shipping company, above whose entrance flew the French tricolour. Banfield's secretary, another handsome lady, sensed my lack of fluency in Italian and chose to speak French.

'Have you read any Gide?' she asked, fixing my eyes with hers in a way to which I was not accustomed in England. I cannot now remember what I replied but it obviously exhausted my limited existentialist French. She showed me a copy of *L'Ecole des Femmes* by Molière and urged me to read it, saying, as her eyes once again fixed mine, that I should find it 'full of insights'. As I digested this advice, I was shown into a large office with three high windows overlooking the calm, almost motionless Adriatic.

I was not at all sure what to expect this hero of the Great War to be like. In 1979, he was the last living former Imperial Austrian officer to have been decorated personally by the Emperor Franz Josef. In 1917 he had been awarded the Empire's highest award for chivalry, the Order of

Maria Theresa, by the last Habsburg Emperor, Charles. This decoration originated in the great battles of the Seven Years' War and automatically conferred elevation to the ranks of the nobility.

The man now opposite me was smaller than I had imagined. His eyes twinkled with a penetrating blue. His face was still boyish, strong and handsome, in many ways English in countenance and colouring, yet softened by more Austrian motifs – generous lips, aquiline nose. His style was old Triestine: lowest of low keys, courteous, diffident and charming. One hand easily waved me to a chair while the other pulled out a deep draw in his desk to reveal two glasses and a bottle of brandy. This was a local drink, for the distillery – in those days still run by the formidable Baroness Stock, another old Austrian aristocrat – was less than two miles away along the coast from where we were sitting.

'Some brandy, Mr Bassett?' It was 9.15 in the morning. Banfield's English was faultless and he enjoyed flitting from English to German, lapsing occasionally into Triestine dialect whose dry, open vowels were beginning to become familiar to me. He also spoke the Viennese German of the nobility with its clipped past participles and drawling French adjectives. Things or con-

17

ditions were either *'miserabel'* (poor) or (better) *'akzeptabel'*. Here, for the first though not the last time, I would absorb the unspoken expectation of that old Austrian generation that fluency in six languages (with perhaps a working knowledge of another three) was perfectly usual. The English predilection for studying languages at university, had I had the temerity to refer to it, would probably have been considered curious.

Our conversation meandered over the fields of finance, geopolitics, the folly of nationalism and the old Emperor Franz Josef, whom Banfield recalled as animated and enquiring, keen to know all about the new 'war in the air'. Austria would need men like Banfield, the old Emperor had said, 'long after this war is over.'

Spring approached, and I was eager to move into a flat closer to the town centre. As usual, Myrta came to the rescue, promising to introduce me to an old countess who often rented the spare room of her apartment in the Via XXX Ottobre, not far from the church of San Antonio.

The countess agreed to see us after lunch one day. As Myrta and I slowly ascended the large, darkly lit staircase, a ghostly voice echoed down the stairs urging us to mount the steps unhurriedly. I dimly made out the source of this encouragement, a small head high above us, smiling benevolently. As we reached the second floor, I saw across the landing a lady in her late seventies with a compassionate face, who regarded me intently. 'Welcome to Trieste,' she announced in a soft Austrian drawl.

A brass plaque with the name 'Korvin' in faint Jugendstil letters adorned the door and indeed, beyond it, not much appeared to have changed since Imperial times. A kitchen of almost Balkan primitiveness with an old gas oven occupied one corner; a small room with a window onto a wall functioned as a kind of bathroom, though the tin bowls stacked up beside the bath hinted at challenges with running water. Disorder was kept in check by phalanxes of old wooden furniture, dark and heavy in the style of the Neo-Renaissance. On a hexagonal Ottoman table, a white-marble Art Nouveau figure of a lady stretched out her arms towards us.

'You know how difficult it is these days to find... *Personal.*' This last word Blanka (as she insisted we call her) pronounced *'Perr-so-naal'* in the nasal Austrian manner. It was explained that a 'temporary' shortage of servants was responsible for the little touches of untidiness. Both

Myrta and I unhesitatingly acquiesced to this happy fiction, which the manners of old Central Europe somehow made much easier to accept smilingly and without question, which would not have been the case among the potato-and-whisky[5] Protestant certainties of the north.

Myrta had explained earlier that Blanka had experienced both the best and the worst of life. Fêted as a great beauty in the Thirties – James Stewart had invited her to Hollywood – she had first married an Italian prince and then, on his sudden death, become involved with the finance minister of King Zog of the Albanians. The arrival of the communists in Tirana towards the end of the 1939–45 war had brought incarceration and torture. Years later, long after Blanka had died, I was given in Albania a photograph taken of her after her release from prison in the 1950s, in which she looked emaciated and exhausted.

On this day, however, our conversation was limited to polite superficialities. Would she mind if I practised the French horn? 'Of course. How nice. I love ze Corn.' Myrta emptied the cup of Turkish coffee we were served, made her excuses and left us to agree the formalities. My room was

---

5 'Out of a gothic North, the pallid children / Of a potato, beer-or-whisky / Guilt culture' (W.H. Auden, 'Good-Bye to the Mezzogiorno')

generous, with a single long window looking across the road to an old palazzo of the Josephinian era, complete with Biedermeier columns and a grand pediment. Its dignity was only slightly compromised by a small illuminated neon sign on the *piano nobile* that flickered, rather coyly, 'Club Mexico'.

As spring turned to summer, the value of the heavy curtains and dark shutters became daily more apparent. I became used to sleeping less and waking up to see from my window Blanka in her stylish dressing gown pacing the balcony, enjoying the early morning breeze. If, very rarely, I needed to get up early to catch a train to the university of Udine, where I taught two days a week, Blanka would enter my room with a cup of strong Turkish coffee, theatrically announcing that I must 'Stay up!' as 'The fleet! *Die Flotte!*' was weighing anchor. It resonated with her – this daughter of an Imperial Austrian naval officer, who had been educated in Constantinople as a small girl before going to the prestigious Sacred Heart convent of Pressbaum near Vienna in 1916 – that the surest way to get an Englishman out of bed must be to invoke the all-powerful Royal Navy.

Blanka had very few friends. A sister – Christa

Spun-Strizic – lived in Zagreb, where, despite the restrictions of the communist Tito regime, she enjoyed a large apartment of considerable old Austrian splendour, surrounded by portraits of Habsburg generals and an army of servants.

Gianpaulo Tamaro was a jovial lawyer who often drove Blanka, at great speed in his Alfa-Romeo, to the Croatian capital. As I got to know Blanka better, I discovered that Tamaro had played a not insignificant role in preparing the legal battle with the Albanian authorities to allow Blanka to leave that benighted country in the early 1950s, after her term of incarceration. What possessed Tamaro to take up her case I never knew; he had stumbled across it during his student days. In any event, the two had become firm friends since Blanka's return to Trieste, always joking and laughing when they were together.

Not that Blanka ever seemed gloomy or melancholy to me. Despite, or perhaps because of, her difficulties, she exuded contagious well-being and calm. Although she was always scathing about Trieste's commercial heritage – 'The Austrians simply said, "Come to Trieste, make money and we don't ask any questions"' – she possessed Olympian detachment from worldly things, along with an acute power of observation and humane curiosity that enabled her to converse freely with anyone.

Unsurprisingly, given her life, she was a devout Catholic. She always maintained that prayer had kept her alive in Albania. It was one of her maxims that 'prayer always takes you higher'. This *Pietas Austriaca*, with its unhesitating belief in ritual, Marian devotion and divine providence, so alien to the conventional English sensibility, was a link with the Austria of the Counter Reformation. Its simple Jesuitical verities could still engage the most sophisticated of modern thinkers. One evening, after reading aloud Aldous Huxley's advice that a man in love should never choose a wife because he is 'like a blind man buying a painting', I asked Blanka what she thought of this. Blanka paused for thought before saying, with an air of affable finality: 'Very interesting idea, but what about divine inspiration?'

Some years later I would meet an Albanian lady who remembered finding Blanka, soon after her release from prison, wandering around the Tirana market telling astonished passers-by that she was leaving for Italy. When asked who had told her this, she replied, according to this

Albanian witness, 'A voice on the nearby hill of St Mark.' This was six months before Tamaro, still unknown to her, tracked her case down. She left with one of the last groups of Italians to be allowed out by the Hoxha regime.

One loyal friend of Blanka's nearer to Trieste was His Serene Highness, Raimondo Principe della Torre e Tasso, a scion of the Thurn and Taxis family who lived in the nearby castle of Duino. Early one morning in October, Blanka gleefully announced over breakfast that we had been invited for drinks at the castle and that we would be heading off there by bus later that afternoon. I was instructed to find a tie worthy of an *Empfang*[6]. From a large Victorian Huntley & Palmers biscuit tin, some boot polish and a small velvet cushion were extracted to assist further our sartorial preparations.

At Duino, on arrival at the castle lodge, Blanka led me up the hill, past the liveried staff, to the medieval *castello* I had so often admired from the train between Venice and Trieste. The saturnine prince greeted us with magnificent joviality. I was not sure what sort of account Blanka had given of me but it was immediately clear that there had been, in traditionally baroque fashion,

6 A reception

the usual generous and unmerited hyperbole.

'How is Prince Charles?' our host inquired in solid English as I took in his splendid striped shirt, with its princely coronet under which his initials seemed at first glance to spell out, rather alarmingly, TNT. Blanka whispered, 'Don't forget to call him *Durchlaucht!* Your Grace!' This word worked like a spell and the conversation moved fluently to other things of which I had slightly more knowledge.

The room we were in looked out over the sea from a considerable height and Blanka urged our host to show us the *Felsen*, the dramatic rocky cliffs below, like jagged white teeth. Here, one windswept morning, Rainer Maria Rilke had composed the first of his great *Duino Elegies*.

As we stepped back from the view below, I noticed the gentle and feminine decoration of the room, with its striped wallpaper and pictures of Vienna, foils to the wildness below. The glasses chinked, there was the habitual gossip about some errant mutual acquaintance and, two hours later, with the sun setting over the autumnal horse chestnuts, we walked down the hill to the village and took the bus back to Trieste.

It would be nearly seventeen years before I

stood in that room at Duino again, this time alone, looking out onto the *Felsen*. That view was unchanged. But inside, large empty squares of faded colour revealed where the paintings of Vienna had hung until only a few days earlier. Nearly everything in this room had been carried away, dispersed by the auctioneer's unsentimental hammer. The jovial prince had died and his family, who had enjoyed this sublime property for centuries, were departing, surrendering the patrimony of hundreds of years in the face of 'the financial challenges of globalisation'. This room, which in '79 had resounded to so much jollity and laughter, was now cold and deserted. From the great window I saw again the rocks and remembered how Blanka had seized my arm in her excitement at the sublime view. Perhaps I was now beginning to understand what Rilke meant when, at this very spot, he had written, *'Ein jeder Engel ist schrecklich.'*[7]

Banfield too had died, though not before he had visited Vienna one last time to be celebrated in the Astoria hotel by Austria's greatest living military historians, a distinguished silver-and-grey figure dressed in a double-breasted suit. He seemed like a sepia photograph in which the

---

[7] 'Every angel is terrible.' (*Duino Elegies,* First Elegy)

only splash of colour was the small red-and-white ribbon of his Maria Theresa Order buttonhole, emblem of the military brotherhood of which he was the last surviving member.

The eclectic salon of the Bar Danubio had also dispersed. Even Voghera and Kern, who seemed for so many years always to be available for coffee and conversation, were now only happy memories of wise insights, or, in Kern's case, of dazzling insults. As for Blanka, it seemed appropriate somehow that she and Tamaro, whose lives had been so intertwined by destiny, should have found death together at precisely the same instant when, one winter evening on the drive back from Zagreb to Trieste, Tamaro's Alfa-Romeo crashed at high speed in the dense fog.

From the Molo Audace, the Triestine sky remains the bluest in the Adriatic, its infinite horizon a reminder that it is not time which is moving but rather we, the fleeting protagonists of our own modest epics, who never stand still.